TO:

FROM:

DATE:

WORDS OF PRAISE FOR
ALL ALONG YOU WERE BLOOMING

"There is abundant compassion and kindness in Morgan's beautiful words. She writes and creates art as a loving act of service, and her readers can feel that love on every page. Morgan's words will give you ownership of the life you've lived, enrich the life you have, and expand your possibilities for the life you want. She has a gift for making the toughest parts of life feel sacred and manageable and for making the good seem even more joyful. Her book will be a treasured companion for anyone who wants to live with more self-kindness and depth and will surely be revisited for many years to come. We are so lucky to have a creative soul like Morgan guiding us through life!"

—Mari Andrew, Author of *New York Times* bestseller *Am I There Yet?*

"Morgan is beyond talented with words that touch the heart, and this work is an extension of her unique gift. Every page is full of life and vibrant color, and each word is presented creatively and beautifully. This book is one of a kind and will leave you feeling simultaneously uplifted and challenged."

—Jordan Lee Dooley, National Bestselling Author of *Own Your Everyday*

"Every page of *All Along You Were Blooming* is visually stunning and profoundly evocative. Morgan Harper Nichols blends vulnerable reflections with ethereal elegance as she layers illustrations beneath her vulnerable poetry and honest musings on love, life, and spirituality. Prepare to have your heart opened by these delightful ruminations and your imagination inspired by her captivating images."

—Christopher L. Heuertz, Author of *The Sacred Enneagram: Finding Your Unique Path to Spiritual Growth*

"*All Along You Were Blooming* is magic. Sure, it's a book—paper, binding, words and all—but it's actually more of a beautiful and brilliant beam of warm sunlight."

—RYAN O'NEAL, SINGER-SONGWRITER, SLEEPING AT LAST

"I first discovered Morgan's work when a close friend of mine printed out a part of her poem on a card and sent it to me:

You are wrapped in
endless,
boundless,
grace.

Morgan had distilled a biblical truth into something clear, profound, and eternally uplifting. I knew there and then that I had to work with her. She has since created prose for *Esquire* that speaks to men in a way that evokes and inspires; challenging our readers to build a life with purpose.

This collection of poetry and prose by Morgan continues her *reason d'être*—to create work that gives hope. And I'm sure, just like me, you'll find yourself taking pages from this book and placing them at your desk as a daily reminder: you are wrapped in endless, boundless grace. It's like a hot water bottle for your weary soul."

—NORMAN TAN, EDITOR-IN-CHIEF OF *ESQUIRE* SINGAPORE

"Morgan [Harper Nichols] lives, writes, and designs with the intention to meet you where you are while simultaneously offering a brand-new perspective. As her younger sister, I've experienced this firsthand with the way her captivating artwork and encouraging words filled our home. This book is a front-row seat to those endless expressions, beautifully laced in grace and truth."

—JAMIE-GRACE, 2X GRAMMY NOMINATED SINGER/
SONGWRITER, HOST OF *THE JAMIE GRACE PODCAST*

"Morgan always has the right words to say—and the perfect way of beautifully sharing those words in a way that speaks to my soul. And obviously countless others. I got goosebumps reading this book and look forward to picking it up for encouragement day after day for years to come."

—BRANDEN HARVEY, FOUNDER OF THE *GOODNEWSPAPER*
AND HOST OF THE PODCAST *SOUNDS GOOD*

"Morgan's tender, intentional words feel like the salve our aching hearts all need reminding of. She is a mirror of the inherent goodness, worth, and divinity inside of all of us."

—RUTHIE LINDSEY, SPEAKER AND COHOST
OF THE *UNSPOKEN* PODCAST

"Have you ever read something and asked yourself, *How did she know?* That's Morgan's gift. Morgan Harper Nichols is changing the game for women around the world today. Her art speaks to the masses while simultaneously making you feel seen, heard, and understood as a human being. As a masterful encourager, permission granter, and inspirer, Morgan's voice reaches readers with heartfelt encouragement and hope. With each thoughtful word, Morgan makes you feel more enough and less alone, and the world needs more of that."

—JENNA KUTCHER, HOST OF THE *GOAL DIGGER* PODCAST

"With rare talent, Morgan Harper Nichols invites us into the reality that we're magnificently loved—even while in process. *All Along You Were Blooming* provides both a balm to weary souls who need to hear they don't have to have it all figured out, as well as a gentle encouragement to take the next right step. Morgan's work reminds us that the magic of growth happens in process; and though it won't be easy, each of us is worth the time it takes to bloom."

—AUNDI KOLBER MA, LPC, THERAPIST
AND AUTHOR OF *TRY SOFTER*

"Morgan's words have a way of reaching into your soul and making you feel completely seen. This book will bring you comfort and peace and will make you feel not alone in this emotional human existence. This will spark inspiration and hope in your life."

—CAITLIN CROSBY BENWARD, FOUNDER OF THE GIVING KEYS

"Morgan Harper Nichols has an incredible gift for speaking the truth that we are all trying to find the words to say. Each page is a beautiful pump of bravery and courage through both her writing and her art."

—ASHLEY LeMIEUX, AUTHOR OF *BORN TO SHINE*, SPEAKER, ENTREPRENEUR

"All Along You Were Blooming provides stabilizing prose that will capture the hearts of those who crave stability, peace, and assurance in these uncertain times."

—EKEMINI UWAN, PUBLIC THEOLOGIAN

"Morgan's work reminds everyone who encounters it to lean in and trust the process. This book is a great reminder to bloom and flourish, despite the hardships that may arise. The world is lucky to have a collection as stunning as this one."

—ALEXANDRA ELLE, AUTHOR AND POET

"Morgan's voice is inspiring millions. Her poetry and art embody a truth that we all deserve to hear."

—MILES ADCOX, CEO OF ONSITE

"Love and beauty pour from the words and art on the pages. Morgan's book is a balm for healing, a step toward joy, and a reminder to care for and be gentle with ourselves and each other. The world and my soul could always use more of that!"

—AMENA BROWN, POET, AUTHOR OF *HOW TO FIX A BROKEN RECORD*, HOST OF *HER WITH AMENA BROWN PODCAST.*

ALL ALONG YOU WERE BLOOMING

thoughts for boundless living

MORGAN HARPER NICHOLS

To my family, teachers, and friends around the world
whose lives have enriched my own in countless ways.
The pages of this book are inspired by the stories
you have so generously shared with me. Thank you.

ZONDERVAN

All Along You Were Blooming

© 2020 by Morgan Harper Nichols

This title is also available as a Zondervan ebook.

This title is also available as a Zondervan audio book.

Requests for information should be addressed to:

Zondervan, *3900 Sparks Dr. SE, Grand Rapids, Michigan 49546*

ISBN 978-0-310-45407-6 (HC)

Scripture quotations are taken from the Holy Bible, New International Version®, niv®. Copyright © 1973, 1978, 1984, 2011 by Biblica, Inc.® Used by permission of Zondervan. All rights reserved worldwide. www.Zondervan.com. The "NIV" and "New International Version" are trademarks registered in the United States Patent and Trademark Office by Biblica, Inc.®

Art direction: Jennifer Showalter Greenwalt

Interior design: Mallory Collins and Morgan Harper Nichols

Printed in China

22 23 24   DSC   12

INTRODUCTION

As a quieter, introverted type, I often thought that unless I had a certain charisma about myself, I could never show up in the world in a way that truly matters. Feeling this way sent me inward, deep inside my journals where I would create a song, a poem, or a painting that communicated all the things I could never quite figure out how to say during the day. With everything I created, there was always a tinge of self-doubt that kept me wondering, *Do I have anything worth sharing?*

A few years ago, on a particularly cold autumn day, I found myself in a pit of self-doubt. Yet I was beginning to realize that if I ever wanted to grow, I couldn't stay there. I realized that I could spend the rest of my life doubting myself, or I could make the brave decision to work through self-doubt and allow myself to be stretched in ways I had not been before. I took a deep breath and wrote an Instagram message to the people who were following my work. I invited them to tell me their stories and, one by one, I would write something for each of them. I began this project that same day, and I haven't looked back. Everything I began to share with the world was created with one person in mind at a time, and this book was written in the same way.

It is my hope that with the words and art you find on these pages, you feel spoken to and you feel heard. I hope you are able to walk away from this book seeing a flicker of Light at midnight reminding you that all along you were blooming. In a world that often seems too crowded or busy to notice beautiful things or make meaningful connections, there is still room for each of us to grow in the ways we were meant to. May each page remind you of this truth.

FOR THE HEART

WHAT YOU FEEL

1

FOR THE MIND

WHAT YOU THINK

51

FOR THE BODY

WHAT YOU DO

95

FOR THE SOUL

WHO YOU ARE

139

FOR THE HEART

WHAT YOU FEEL

Hold tight to hope,
amidst all unanswered questions
for even in uncertainty,
there is strength to be found,
and grace will still abound
in what you do not understand.

Under blue skies,
on cracked rocks,
in dry heat,
in desert land,
grace is the hand that is never out of reach
reminding you:
you are not weak
because you are lonely.

And even if you have heard the word *grace*
over and over again
and you think you already know what it means
there is grace for that, too,
humbly reminding you of its endlessness,
and how much you need it
when you are lost in the wilderness.

So do not be disheartened,
when the landscape is working against you,
and do not think that you have failed
when you are not sure you'll make it through;
for this glorious unmerited favor called grace
will meet you where you are,
giving you peace amidst your restlessness,
and safety from alarm.

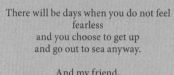

There will be days when you do not feel
fearless
and you choose to get up
and go out to sea anyway.

And my friend,
let me tell you,
that is what it means to be brave.
It is that gentle shove toward the water
that says "I will go,
and I will go afraid."

It is not a feeling.
It is not a thought.
It is that inward wind that pulls you out of sleep
and says "I will go forth,
with all I have now:
a breath, a dozen steps,
and a pocket full of fears,
but no matter what tries to pull me back,
I will find the strength to be here."

LEAVE ROOM FOR BEAUTIFUL INTERRUPTION;
LIGHT, UNEXPECTED,
ARRIVING IN THE MIDDLE OF THE NIGHT.
FOR PERHAPS HERE IN THE DARKNESS,
YOU WILL START TO SEE THE REALITY
OF ALL THE WALLS
YOU HAVE BUILT UP
AROUND YOURSELF
AND HOW
THEY HAVE KEPT YOU
FROM LIVING.

FOR WHEN YOU ARE BROKEN,
IT MIGHT SEEM LIKE THE ONLY THING THERE IS TO DO
IS TO HEAD OUT
IN SEARCH OF THE LOVE OF ANOTHER,
BUT WHAT IF,
INSTEAD OF LOOKING ELSEWHERE,
YOU LOOKED RIGHT HERE AT THE WALLS
YOU HAVE BEEN HIDING BEHIND FOR YEARS.

FOR THE WALLS YOU BUILT
TO PROTECT YOURSELF,
GAVE YOU A NARROW VIEW OF THE WORLD.
THEY STUNTED YOUR LIMBS,
AND YOU STRUGGLED TO BREATHE.

SO MAYBE, NOW IS THE TIME
TO ALLOW LIGHT'S INTERRUPTION
POURING IN THROUGH THE CRACKS,
REMINDING YOU OF MEANINGFUL LIFE, ON THE OTHER SIDE.

YOU WERE SEEKING SAFETY,
BUT STAYING BEHIND THESE SELF-MADE WALLS
HAS NEVER BEEN THE WAY.

YOU NEED SOMETHING MORE
TO COMFORT YOU IN BROKENNESS
WHEN THE PAIN IS TALL AROUND YOU,
TO REMIND YOU THAT EVEN HERE,
YOU ARE INFINITELY LOVED.

AND WHEN THESE WALLS COME DOWN,
YOU WILL SEE A BROKEN,
BEAUTIFUL WORLD AROUND YOU
INVITING YOU TO STEP INTO
A DAILY CHANCE
TO LIVE BEYOND
THE BARRIERS OF WHO YOU WERE.

For all those conversations
that happened years ago,
may you know this to be true:
no matter how dark the night,
in the morning, Light pours through,
filling every corner of the room.

For shame has tried to tear
at the very heart of you.
It has sunk your mind
in lying thoughts of
is this still worth living for?

But even though
these thoughts have found you in a weary place,
they do not have the final word.
They do not tell your story.

You are free
to move around the room,
to paint the walls a new color,
and declare there is more to you.

I am not sure who
has made you feel insignificant,
but I can assure you
no matter how you have been made to feel,
your voice deserves to be heard.
Your words are meant to be felt.
And the life that comes out of you
is unique to you and no one else.

You may not have the next few years figured out,
and there are times when you want to speak up
but you do not know how.
But
when the words do finally come
and you find the courage to open up,
your story will not be too much.

I hope you know it is okay to have moments when you do not know what to say. I hope you know in the arms of Love, you have nothing to be ashamed of, even when the questions you are asking have no easy answers. I hope you know you are heard, in the wildest, roaring waves. I hope you know it is okay to lean into the grace that reminds you things will come together in the way they were supposed to.

EVEN IN YOUR
UNCERTAINTY
AND EVEN IN
YOUR WAITING,
YOU HAVE MADE IT
THIS FAR, AND
THAT IS WORTH
CELEBRATING.

You were meant
to give your all,
and you were also meant
to be loved.
You were meant
to have meaningful connection
beyond what you feel
you are worthy of.

So have faith that unmerited favor
has been made available to you,
no matter the heartaches
broken friendships
have brought you.

You are free to forgive
and you are also free
to heal.
You are worthy of love
no matter how anyone else
has made you feel.

Never let anyone who cannot bear your pain make you feel you are unbearable. Not everyone is capable of walking with you, but that does not mean you are not worthy of belonging.

I promise you, there will be other people. There will be other people who are willing to take the time for you. And not because they pity you, but because they believe in the kind of Love that is true. The kind of Love that is not envious. The kind of Love that is not proud. I know you have been let down, but please don't give up on True Love now. It is kind and it is real, no matter how you have been made to feel. Don't give up on Love. Love has not given up on you.

If ever you start to feel weary
of the mundane
and completely restless
in all that has not changed,
and rather numb
to the mention of *grace*,
let today be the day
you make the mindful decision
to find joy in the ordinary places—

the white light between the bedroom blinds,
the taste of rich, dark coffee grinds—

for even though the extraordinary calls you,
and you feel its river running wild through your bones,
and your heart is craving meaning and purpose
on the other side of your unknowns,
there are still these flickers of light and familiar tastes
that are calling your heart to know:
even when you are still,
there are so many ways
to find your way
to gratitude.

when you start to feel
the pull of the past,

and you are helpless
trying to calm
unyielding storms
on your own,

remember
to do the best you can do
while knowing and trusting:
it is not all up to you.

for it is okay,
more than okay
to cast down your burdens
and choose to believe
in healing.

AND SHE KNOWS IN HER SOUL,
WHEN IT COMES TO HER WORTH,
IT DOES NOT MAKE HER WEAK,
FOR NEEDING TO BE REMINDED OF THIS TRUTH:
THIS IS ALL A PART OF BEING GUIDED
RIGHT WHERE SHE NEEDS TO BE,
BEING LIFTED TO THE LIGHT
THAT HER HEART FOREVER NEEDS.

YOUR STORY IS NOT JUST A SHALLOW POOL
COLLECTING A LITTLE RAIN HERE AND THERE
FROM WHAT MAYBE-COULD'VE-SHOULD'VE BEEN.
YOUR STORY IS A SEA, WEIGHTED WITH MYSTERY,
AND WAVE AFTER WAVE IT REVEALS MORE AND MORE,
NO MATTER THE OPPORTUNITIES YOU MISSED
OR LEFT BEHIND ON THE SHORE.

YOUR STORY HAS EVERY OUNCE OF WATER IT NEEDS.
IT IS NOT MISSING ANY LONG-GONE THING.
ALL BY GRACE, IT IS STILL BEING WRITTEN,
IN THE WAY IT WAS MEANT TO BE.

MAY THIS SEASON OF WAITING
  BEND YOUR HEART TOWARD ADVENTURE—
    AN UNEXPECTED INVITATION
      TO JOURNEY
        THROUGH THE WILD OF WHERE YOU ARE.
FOR MAYBE, JUST MAYBE
  YOU DO NOT HAVE TO GO
    VERY FAR
      TO ENCOUNTER SOMETHING MEANINGFUL
        THAT WILL MAKE THE WAIT WORTHWHILE.

16

And how did it feel this morning, still waiting for answers for your pain? Dawn was breaking through, yet no relief, and the sun was only a reminder of time passing by.

You did not wonder *where* you go from here. You wondered *if* you could go from here, and as you struggled to take that breath, you wondered if this is hopelessness.

How did it feel?
How did it feel?

It is okay if there were no words for it,
for language can never possibly hold
this fear, so dark and cold.

And maybe tomorrow
when you look back,
you will find the strength
to tell that story.

But until then, it is okay to be confused. In this stillness, trust that morning still overcomes darkness, and there is a miraculous place you have been invited to. Breathe through.

I feel the gaze of the photograph
peering at me
from the wooden frame
speckled in dust,
but I have to remember:
I am not who I was back then.
Yes, that is my grin, my skin,
but when I look into my own eyes,
I know that I have changed.
I know that even though I still feel traces
of my former self,
I see things differently now.
I have learned not to hide my pain
for fear of what others might say.
I have learned some days will be harder than others,
and that is absolutely okay.
I do not have to be strong all the time.
I am not a burden because I have burdens,
and because there is a lot on my mind.
And maybe not everyone will have time for me,
and maybe there will be people who feel I am too much,
but I have learned that I am still worthy of Love,
and that is more than enough.
And I may not always feel weightless.
I may forget at times that I am free,
but I am learning to fall into grace,
to be led where I am meant to be.

IT IS EASY TO FIX YOUR MIND
ON WHAT FELL APART LAST YEAR,
BUT IN THAT RAW REFLECTION,
BE *gentle* WITH YOUR STORY,
KNOWING THAT THROUGH EVERYTHING
THAT DID OR DID NOT HAPPEN,
THE PIECES WILL STILL COME TOGETHER
AND YOU WILL LOOK BACK AND SEE,
AFTER EVERYTHING,
YOU NOW HAVE *strength*
TO CARRY ON.

IF EVER
YOU START TO FEEL
YOU MUST HOLD THINGS IN,
LET THEM BE
LIFE-GIVING THINGS
THAT REMIND YOU
OF WHO YOU ARE
AND WHO YOU
ARE MEANT TO BE.

Even though
you have learned
the skill of
running on empty,
now is the time
to learn the art
of breathing deep
all over again,
letting no one make you feel
that you cannot show up with the truth
of where you are.

And some may not be ready for your honesty,
but those people are likely equally dissatisfied,
as they have not found the Harvest yet.
So do not be discouraged.
This is no reflection of you.
You are still free to live
your honest story
in the way
it was meant to be written.

You have picked petals
without regard for their stems,
leaving them stripped
of their color,
and when you saw what you had done,
you ran
and ran
and ran
eastbound
through the deserts
to hide,
never to return to flowers again.

A new day is calling you
to stumble into the sunlight,
where old ways
of thinking
are made right
so you can be at peace,
to roam through flowery fields again.
For mercy is always
louder than sharp cries of shame.
It knows where you have been,
but still calls you by your name,
inviting you to step forward with the boldness to begin
a way of living that gives freedom
and to sow new seeds
into the earth again.

It is okay to long for days past. It is natural to feel the imprint of what was, for all you lost is still a part of you. These memories carve their way into your heart, and you do not know how to recover its original form. And even when you try, you cannot shake the old feelings, her words, those photographs . . . but now, even here, after all of these years, you are free to remember, while also moving onward on this path, filled with Light, even if your earliest steps are small.

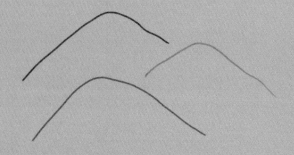

PERHAPS THE TEARS
THAT WELLED IN YOUR EYES TODAY
WERE A WAY
OF LETTING IT ALL GO,
A WAY OF RELEASING
WHAT KEPT YOU
FROM FLYING
ABOVE THE HILLS
THAT ONCE HELD YOU BACK.

It wasn't until she reached the shore
that she realized
she was meant for water.

She no longer yearned
to linger on the lawn
where she had been rejected.

She had reached her end,
and it was there she learned to see,
this was not the end at all.
This was the beginning.

And it would be here,
as the waves rushed in,
she would hear
the sea calling.

She is starting again.
She is coming out to sea to be
a soul
set free
from who she was back then.
And she will go forth in deeper waters,
with hope as the anchor for her soul,
reminding her that it was never other people
that made her feel truly whole,
and all along,
she was called to more,
a glorious life beyond the shore.

SHE NO LONGER HAD THE DESIRE
TO BEND HERSELF INTO
THE FRAME OF PHOTOGRAPHS
WHERE SHE WAS UNWELCOME

Ask yourself
the kinds of questions
that go beyond today's desires,
and dig deeper into the well
of what
you need.

What feelings
do you need to acknowledge?
What fears
have you tucked away?
What things
have you worked so hard for
that have yet to see
the light of day?
What great offering
would you bring the world,
if you had to do it anonymously?
What would you tell your younger self,
to encourage her
to live courageously?

IF YOU HAVE SECRETLY LONGED
FOR SIGNIFICANCE,
THE JOURNEY DOES NOT BEGIN
OUT THERE IN THE WORLD,
BUT DEEP WITHIN,
WHERE YOU EMBRACE
YOUR HONEST SELF.

SO LAY DOWN YOUR WORRY.
LET YOUR HEART BE SEEN.
LET THE OPENNESS REVEAL TO YOU
THE DEEPER LOVE YOU REALLY NEED.

TRUE CONTENTMENT COMES LIKE
UNEXPECTED RAIN, SOAKING INTO
THE SOIL OF THE EARTH'S DRY FLOOR,
REMINDING YOU THAT PERHAPS THERE
IS HOPE FOR THE SEEDS YOU HAVE SOWN.

All she wanted was love—
an adventure with someone
she could count on.
She closed her eyes,
prayed,
took the leap,
and let him in.
It was love.
She thought it was love.
He said it was love.
Is this love?

And though there were wonderful moments,
there were always these lingering thoughts . . .
yes, today was good,
but what about tomorrow?
Where does this lead?
A year from now,
where will we be?

Layer by layer,
things fell apart before her eyes.
He was living for a moment,
while she was hoping for the future.
She was pushed out of his world
and on her own,
trying to gather the pieces of her heart,
and find her way home.

The road back was long.
And it was strange
to go from being in step
with someone,
to journeying on
to the rhythm of her own two feet.
She was walking home
in pieces,
but she realized even though
she was broken, she was still walking home.
She was still headed where she needed to be.

And even though at times
she was certain
he was the worst mistake of her life,
she had gratitude
that after everything,
she had made it out alive.
And now the challenge was
to make it back home.

Having learned and having lived,
she would know Love again,
a deeper, Greater Love that would sustain her broken heart.
Through all that changed
and fell apart before her eyes,
that was the greatest thing
she could have ever learned from this.

DO NOT BE DISMAYED
IF YOU HAVE A BROKEN HEART.
YOU HAVE BEEN PLACED
ON A JOURNEY OF HEALING
WHERE LIGHT SHINES
ON WHAT YOU ARE FEELING:
AN INVITATION TO BELIEVE
IN THE WORST OF THINGS,
THAT CHANGE IS HAPPENING WITHIN YOU
FOR THE BETTER, FOR THE GOOD.

On this road of longing
may you find Belonging
in the arms of grace
and never be the same;
for it is here
you will find
you will be Loved as you are,
you will be Seen as you are,
and you will not be left as you are,
for you have been invited
to go
on this journey of being shaped
into who you were meant to be:
an original work of art.

Through all you are feeling,
and all your inner-longing,
may your soul find comfort
and peace
in Belonging.

Continue to give with good intentions. Love is a good thing, and it is meant to be given. Take a deep breath. The why of your love is what matters.

Perhaps
the vertical
stone
structures
stacked
high
between
you
and others
are not as high and wide as they seem to be,
and they need not keep you
from experiencing
this blessed thing called love.

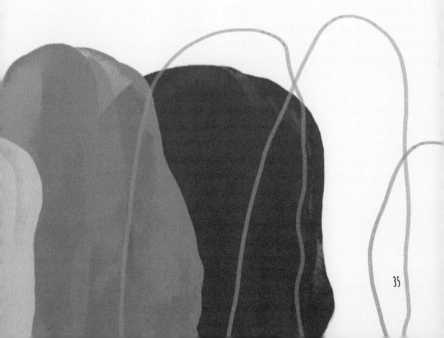

You may have ideas about how others
see you,
but you are not defined
by their perceptions.
You are not an object
under someone else's magnifying glass,
whose only purpose
is to be observed.

You are a living, breathing human being
with a beautiful soul
that is on a hope-anchored journey
of learning what it means to be whole.

The sight of old photographs
sends a sharp pain up your spine.

The days are not going to look the same
from this day forward,
but you will
move forward,
for through all
you have endured,
you have blossomed.
Which was possible
only by the rain.

And perhaps
this is your becoming,
your unfolding
into a grace-filled bloom.

No matter
where the journey takes you,
Light will lead you through.

Let this be
your morning song,
for it is far too easy
to feel alone out here,
in crowded subways
and highways
and trafficked walkways.
They all have a way
of reminding you
of everyone who has moved on
so quickly without you.

But no matter who stays
or who walked away,
remember all the things
they taught you.
Remember
the paths
and the tunnels
you have traveled through.
You learned to see shapes
within the shadows.
You learned to find
the window
and wait for the birds
of the new day to sing,
to remind you
of all that is changing.

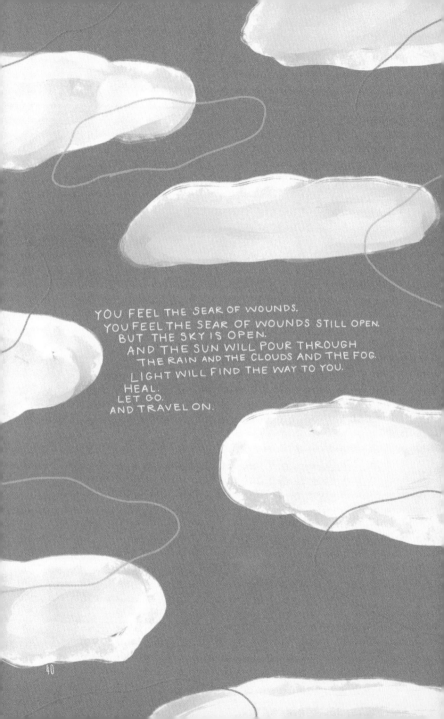

YOU FEEL THE SEAR OF WOUNDS.
YOU FEEL THE SEAR OF WOUNDS STILL OPEN.
BUT THE SKY IS OPEN.
AND THE SUN WILL POUR THROUGH
THE RAIN AND THE CLOUDS AND THE FOG.

LIGHT WILL FIND THE WAY TO YOU.
HEAL.
LET GO.
AND TRAVEL ON.

Sometimes love
is just learning how to stay.
It's not always a grand gesture,
but an inward posture.
And sometimes,
love isn't seen
or appreciated
in the way
you want.
But maybe,
maybe love goes deeper than
what you can see,
and it rattles the soul.

Love is as vast as the ocean,
and we're always only swimming
on the surface of its greatness.
And we may not see
how far our love goes or who it will reach,
but we can always choose to trust.
We need love,
even when we do not know
where the love we are giving
will be received.

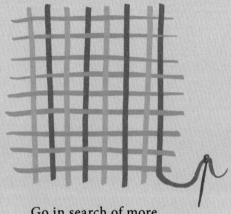

Go in search of more.
When you are unraveling
into severed threads,
new stories are waiting
to be woven,
and you can hope for new beginnings.

This does not mean your journey
will be easy,
but moving forward is an act of faith,
step by step,
even when you cannot imagine
the tapestry on the other side of this.

And no one can take your faith away.

Remember
the heartbreak you saw before your eyes,
the way you felt in the hospital that night,
and that gentle whisper in the soul that you were going to be alright.

Because in your tears and speechless moments
and the times you did not know what to do,
new Life was a path laid out before you,
inviting you to come forth.

Even though you did not know where the path would go.
Even though you did not know where tomorrow would lead.
You were headed in the direction of where you were meant to be.
Above every worry, every doubt, and everything that fell apart,
you were being held together,
making room for an all new start.

And although you came undone,
you now see how far you've come,
and how each day,
each day,
mercy awaits you in the morning.

For whatever pain
lies beneath
your blanket of sorrows,
or the flaws
you have learned to conceal
just to make it
through the day,
it is okay
to grieve
the loss of things
that will never be
the same again.

And this mind of yours
that has pulled you
back to
the worst of things
is the same mind
that is capable
of remembering
the better things:
the sound of green leaves in the spring,
the sight of rain running along the street,
the way laughter can rattle a room.
Years later those senses still find you . . .

They are more than memories.
They are woven
in the layers of your heart,
not hidden
by a blanket of sorrows,
never replaced,
never torn apart.

WHEN SONGS RISE WITHIN ME,
I WILL SING THEM.
EVEN WHEN I AM TIRED,
WEARY AND EXHAUSTED,
I WILL TRUST
THESE MELODIES ARE
MORE THAN MELODIES.
THEY ARE GRACE-FILLED
CADENCES TO REMIND
MY SOUL THROUGH MY
ACHING, THERE IS A
PEACE TO KEEP
ME STEADY... A BALM
FOR MY WOUNDS.

Maybe on the other side of this,
there will be a row of city lights.
Maybe just maybe,
they will light up the sky
and remind us
the world is filled with life.
We have lost more than we could ever imagine,
but now we carry with us
a hope that shines
as bright
as a summer meteor shower,
and love that holds
as steady
as the ground beneath our feet,
and the more we climb
we are beginning to find
just how valuable
life is.

Never carry on
sealed off from life.
Even though
it's difficult to bear,
you are still worthy
of healing and care
and the freedom and peace to move on.

There will be more people,
more places,
peace
beyond understanding.

So hold on to that.
This is how you will be able
to begin to walk on the path,
even if you are still waiting
for answers, closure, clarity.

Even when you cannot discern the terrain
before you take the next step,
now is still the time to go forth,
with an open heart,
knowing that what you have walked through
is valid,
and the experiences
you gather
will be entirely valid too.

CHOOSING TO HAVE JOY
IS NOT NAIVELY THINKING
EVERYTHING
WILL BE EASY.

IT IS COURAGEOUSLY
BELIEVING
THAT THERE IS
STILL HOPE,
EVEN WHEN
THINGS GET HARD.

She is learning to be okay in the mess,
to breathe deep
despite the chaos,
declaring that it will not
overcome her.
For oh,
things have been so heavy lately,
but it has certainly
not defined her.

FEELINGS MEMORIES

Love

Fear

LATE NIGHT THOUGHTS

49

EVEN WHILE YOU WAIT,
YOUR LIFE
IS TAKING SHAPE,
LIKE CLAY
IN THE HANDS
OF THE POTTER.
THERE IS NO NEED
TO BE AFRAID,
FOR WHATEVER
IS BEING SCULPTED
IS WORTHY
AT EVERY STAGE
OF BEING LOVED
AND HELD WITH CARE
FOR EXACTLY
WHAT IT IS.

FOR THE MIND

WHAT YOU THINK

With Light silhouetting my shoulders,
I will push into the dark night,
no longer bound by shadows
that trailed so long behind me.

For they do not tell my story.
They do not hold my truth.
They cannot keep me
from the things
I am meant to do.

Even if my eyes are heavy,
I will push forward with audacity,
and I will rise with strength at dawn.

And when I arrive there, I will smile.
And not the kind of smile
made of gritted teeth,
but the kind that is involuntary and free,
knowing I have made it through to liberty.

For I have known darkness,
and I am learning to be less afraid of it.

If you are swimming in a sea
of unanswered questions,
may you find courage to be silent.
And while the waves
fall over one another
in a splash of black and blue,
slowly drowning out your thoughts
leaving you with nothing else to do
but fall helplessly
under the body
of rolling water,

do not think you must rush on.
It is okay to spend some time here.
It is okay to be the only one here.
The shore is calling, but today, you're in this water.
Find its purpose,
its substance.

Wait in silence.
Fall into a place of listening
and surrender,
and trust that even here,
these whirling waters
will not carry you on forever.
And when the current comes
you will be lifted up,
carried to the shore,
and you will be better
for having been here,
embracing silence amidst
the water's roar.

I hope someday
you know the taste
of early morning mountain air,
and the saltwater waves of the ocean,
and the unexpected bliss of some strange sweet-bitter fruit.
But I hope you also know the taste of hope
on an ordinary Tuesday,
when you do not feel okay,
and you rise up anyway.
Do more
than just visit the world;
belt to the heavens,
listen to the languages of every passerby,
in every single moment
go joy-hunting today.

Despite the pale gray on your horizon,
the gloom of a winter weekday's dawn,

even as you imagine the photographs of a life that could have been,
all the places your mind has wandered
and the stories you had hoped
would end a little differently,

you are still not as lost as you think you are,
you are here, for a reason, to make the most of it.

Listen out for the low-pitched song of the bluebird,
the rustling leaves,
the sound of rain.
Listen for any little reminder of Life,
feel it call you by your name.
Consider the small and nearly missed,
consider the bold, unanimously grand,
consider it all something
worth tasting and cherishing,
making the most of your days at hand.

Consider it a natural thing
if this way of living
takes some patterning
and getting used to,
for this is an unfolding
of a novel-length awakening
of seeing what has always
been calling you.

final moments
between breaths
between midnight and mornings,
when no one is speaking
and no one is singing
but God-Sent-Love is breathing.

WHILE WE ARE TRYING TO MAKE SENSE OF THINGS, MAY WE LEARN TO MAKE PEACE WITH THINGS.

You find yourself
beneath a canopy of trees
with broken branches,
covered with moss tangled at your knees.

Rest assured
the forest does not crawl on forever.

But you must begin the journey
here.

For this is the time,
this is the time to come alive,
to walk tall with a beating heart
and wide-open midday eyes,
to surrender,
here in the green,
for you are still free
to travel free,
without knowing
everything,
humbly following the traces of daylight,
even though the path is unmarked,
even though this was not a favored start,
this is your only Hope
to make it through

precisely here,
pushing through the land of the unknown
you will find your home
in Hope.

So for now,
while you are here,
turn your attention
to the lessons of strength
this present forest offers.

I CANNOT TELL YOU
    THE COLOR OF TOMORROW'S SUNRISE
        OR WHAT HUES WILL BURN
            LIKE LEAVES BEFORE YOUR EYES.

I CANNOT TELL YOU
    WHICH PLANTS IN YOUR GARDEN
    WILL BLOOM BEFORE OTHERS
        OR WHICH ONES YOU WILL HAVE TO PRUNE
        AND WAIT FOR A SEASON LONGER,
        BUT I CAN TELL YOU,
        TOMORROW IS ON ITS WAY.
YOU WILL STEP INTO AN ALL-NEW DAY,
AWAKE.

Shadows
fall like midnight
on your shoulders,
but those shadows will have no grip on you
for they are doomed
to be drowned out by Light.

And you might feel their heaviness
weighing down on your knees,
making it harder
to walk,
to breathe,
but you will be alright,
for you still are learning
what it means to be strong.

You are still a capable, thriving being,
at a slower, shadow-lined pace.

You might feel
overwhelmed
beneath
this canopy
of endless trees,
but if you choose to keep going,
you will soon find the clearing,
an open field
with room
to rest
before you rise and begin again.

For even though
restless questions
crowd your midnight-wondering,
every breath
is a step
in the direction of morning.

Let go
to grab hold
of tomorrow's possibility,
and try again,
try again.

SO WHEN YOU
ASK HOW I'VE BEEN,
I WRAP MY WORDS
IN TODAY'S BEAUTIFUL TRUTH
THAT I AM NOT
WHO I WAS
BACK THEN.
I WILL NOT JUSTIFY
THIS SELF-EVIDENT REALITY
THAT GRACE
HAS CHANGED
MY VIEW.

Here's to more vivid dreams,
when-you-are-sleeping dreams and
wide-awake middle-of-the-day dreams
that make your heart fall in love
in an instant.

Because lately, these hills you have been climbing
have woven weariness into your bones,
driving you further and further from home,
and as much as you want to believe
the terrain will even itself out,
you have persisting doubts
and gray scale fears
that the road signs
will be obstructed
by the rain
and you will be stuck here,

estranged in an unknown place.

So when you are struggling to keep climbing,
and the wind has blown you to your knees,
and any hope you had
fell through the cracks
of the earth,
dream
of the tree-lined clearing up ahead
you have yet to see.

Have the audacity
to keep dreaming
in full color, come undone,
letting hope have its way.

And whenever
she starts to forget
the story of her original bloom,
the flowers of this green earth remind her
she too will spring up from the ground
again.
Gravity will not restrain her,
for the sun and rainfall
will propel her
up
from gritty soil
into open morning air,
and Light will meet her there
and she will
begin
to unfold
in the way
she is meant to.

When it's 2 a.m.
and the room
is lined
with shadows,
turn your eyes
toward the window—
to the little light burn of
the street lamp
the white star
the flickering red light of the airplane passing by . . .
breathe deep, breathe deep,
it is okay
to feel a little out of place
in this dark and restless space
and come falling,
falling
into grace.

And know this is still true:
Lo, I am
with you
until the end of end of earth,
even at restless 2 a.m.'s,
even when it hurts.

So turn on the music,
open the book,
you do not have to count the hours.
You may have lost your share of sleep,
but Light will never lose the glory,

and no matter how long these late nights last,
the sun is on the way
with mercy in the morning.

I believe
there is a time for everything under the sun.
A time to live, a time to die,
a time to rise, to dream, to become . . .
to find room for me
in the most crowded spaces of my mind,
to see there is still time
for me to slow down,
process things,
and let Ecclesiastes sing to me:

you may have come undone,
but there is a time under the sun,
for everything,
absolutely everything.

You do not have to live afraid.
You do not have to live in an overgrown garden
of weeds
that have no place.

Every fear you have known
did not come here alone,
it came with its own story
welling up from the past.

Never let fear make a home in your garden.
It is a weed,
but you are free to yank it up,
you are free to speak with fire:
"enough is enough."

For this garden of your life
is the place where flowers grow,
and they are not only beautiful—
they are powerful,
releasing breath into the air around them.
Pause
and exhale.

PERHAPS THIS IS THE SEASON
    TO STEP FULLY INTO THE BEAUTIFUL REALITY
    OF WHAT IT MEANS TO BE FREE:
        BRAVE AND ADVENTUROUS
        AND READY FOR THE JOURNEY
    OF LEARNING AND GROWING,
    OF LIVING AND KNOWING
    YOU DO NOT HAVE TO HAVE EVERY ANSWER
    TO BREATHE DEEP AND KEEP GOING.

KEEP YOUR EYES ON THE LIGHT
SPILLING OUT ONTO THE ENTRYWAYS,
SEEPING INTO CORNERS,
HOVERING OVER THE FLOORBOARDS,
PIERCING THROUGH THE WINDOWPANES,
ALL THE WAYS IT RUNS WILD
UNDER THIS SHRINKING ROOF
AS A REMINDER
THAT EVEN HERE,
LIGHT IS YOUR GUIDE.

Remember this place
in the years to come.
Remember the streetlight,
flickering and dim.
And that silvery car
parked
awaiting the traffic light,
reflecting back the red hues
so typical of
that season of life.
It will pass on,
in time,
it passes on.

Are they residents,
or are they
merely passing through?

Oh, these seemingly insignificant
moments of light,
I am still
grateful for you.

八

Dive in
beyond the reef.

And what will you call it?
What will you name
this grand adventure?

Will you call it
"Into the deep,"
"The day I finally learned to breathe,"
"The strength I did not know I would need,"
or will you simply call it
"Be"?
For after all,
this is what
you are doing:
discovering
the courage
living inside of you
is not as distant
as it seemed.

No matter how this season ends,
you will walk away knowing
what you did not know back then.
This year will not end like last year,
nor any other year before.

IF EVER YOU HAVE BEEN AFRAID TO FLY
FOR FEAR OF WHERE YOU'D LAND,
AND YOU HAVE STRUGGLED FINDING PEACE
IN WHAT YOU DO NOT UNDERSTAND,
KNOW THAT TRUSTING IS BETTER THAN KNOWING
THERE IS GROUND BENEATH YOUR FEET
BECAUSE, MY DEAR, COURAGE IS FOUND
IN BELIEVING BEYOND WHAT YOU CAN SEE.

May you never forget all of the people you met
who planted seeds of hope
in your life
when you least expected it.
May you never forget
the garden
that still bloomed
even after your driest seasons.

No matter how big or small,
these people and these places
have been part of it all:
season into season.

Together, you have watched dead things come to life,
day by day, flower by flower.

Take a look around
at what is still growing:
    a tree outside your window
    your collection of books
    a friendship
    hope

For by grace you will grow
into who you were meant to be,
and you will arrive,
and thrive,
in due season
together.

At the right time,
every broken thing
will come together for the good.
You are more than your
failures,
successes,
more than your fears.
And far beyond the surface
of your desires,
there is a truer reason
why you are still here.
If you find yourself struggling
to see past your imperfections
because you cannot figure out how
what's torn apart can come together,
may you know in your soul
that the answer is not found in thinking,
feeling,
doing,
but in trusting in what is Greater than you.

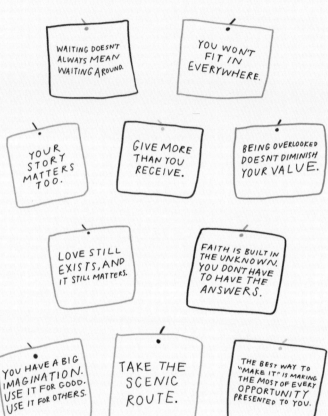

Some fears are like droughts
that roll in over mountains
stripping the earth
of the lush green and soft soil
that once promised
fruitful life,
sending your tired eyes searching
for hope
in what has become
the most hopeless place.

But it is in these desperately barren landscapes
you come to learn:
this Glorious Living Water
running wild through your veins
is entirely
unafraid
of the dry, scorched place of your fears.

So take heart when fear is raging.
Seek courage over control.
Learn to let go into the wild of things,
learn to grow as things unfold.

TAKE HEART,
  TAKE HEART,
    DO NOT BE AFRAID.
      THE FUTURE MAY BE UNCERTAIN,
      BUT THERE IS NO NEED
        TO HIDE AWAY.
        EVERY DAY IS AN OPPORTUNITY
      TO COURAGEOUSLY SHOW UP,
    EVEN WHEN YOU DO NOT FEEL EQUIPPED,
  OR THAT YOU WILL BE ENOUGH.
LET GRACE SURPRISE YOU,
  SETTING FIRE TO YOUR BONES,
    STRENGTHENING YOUR MIND
      IN THE WILD OF YOUR UNKNOWNS.

Be at peace in the mystery.
You can thrive in the mystery,
feel free and safe in mystery,
assured the ground beneath your feet
is safe and ever sturdy.
Not everything can be put into words.

A mystery-ridden life is still filled with Light,
and it is okay
to have days
where you are still learning

what that looks like.

May this be the season
OF COURAGEOUS PURSUIT:
to fully enjoy the present moment
RIGHT IN FRONT OF YOU,
no longer restrained
BY HEAVY MIND
and things to do,
CHOOSING TO BELIEVE
with bold faith
TODAY IS WORTH
a long and loving look.

Make a ~~practice~~ of resting.

There will be mountains,
coastlines,
and sunsets over power lines,
and there will also be moments
when you are lost in your room
of journals
filled with unanswered prayers
and a wall of photographs
that taunt you
with cold, distant stares—

but slowly and surely,
you find
graceful strength
to press into the moment
and come alive within it,
to turn to a blank page
and start writing again,
to remember the way you felt
when those photographs
were first taken,
realizing that nothing
stays the same,
but even though
things have changed,
you can see old things as new
in the most ordinary rooms.

Even the dull moments
that make you long
to be elsewhere,
will prepare you
for where you want to be,
and you will have gratitude
when you arrive there.
Find the music
in the noise around you,
shuffling footsteps,
distant chatter,
the sound of doors
swinging open and closed,
the buzz of a phone,
the occasional laughter . . .
You may not have chosen
your surroundings,
but you can choose
to find life in them.

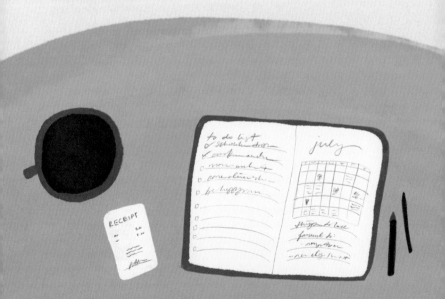

When that inner
critical voice
decides
to speak,
it must not
lead the way.
It does not speak
for how you have grown.
It does not speak
for when you fell.
It does not speak
for where you are going
and the story
your life tells.

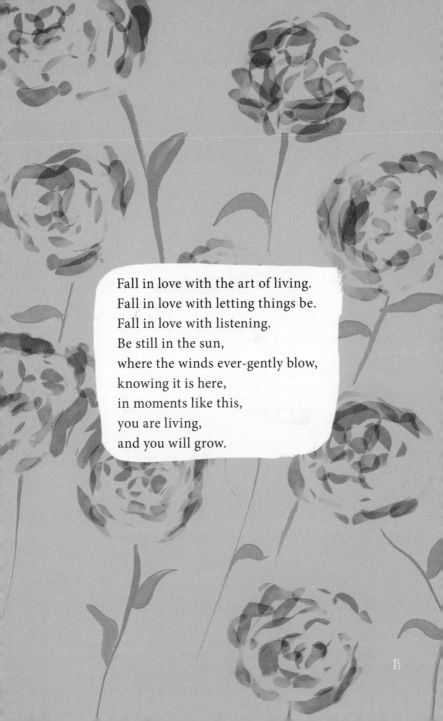

Fall in love with the art of living.
Fall in love with letting things be.
Fall in love with listening.
Be still in the sun,
where the winds ever-gently blow,
knowing it is here,
in moments like this,
you are living,
and you will grow.

YOU ARE FREE
TO LAY YOUR
BURDENS DOWN,
COMING ALIVE
RIGHT HERE,
RIGHT NOW.

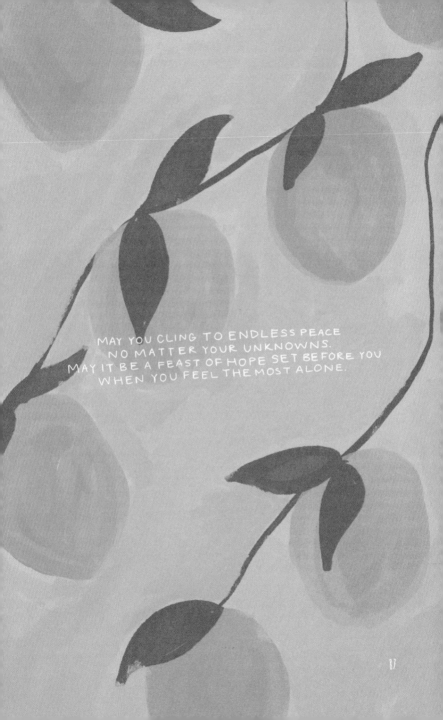

MAY YOU CLING TO ENDLESS PEACE
NO MATTER YOUR UNKNOWNS.
MAY IT BE A FEAST OF HOPE SET BEFORE YOU
WHEN YOU FEEL THE MOST ALONE.

I do not know
what has left you empty
or made you feel
like you could never be
enough—

that your love
was not enough.

But I can promise you,
as long as your heart is beating,
you are meant to be
on this earth, and you have more love to give,
and there is more love
to be given to you.

When you are exhausted
trying to choose
which door
is best
for you,
and you fear
that if you do not make the right choice
at a wall of a hundred doors,
slow down and remember,
within the Light,
you will not fail.

Once you begin to see
how Light spills through
no matter which door you choose,
you will have confidence
to meet any challenges that lie ahead.
And even when your mind
is filled with questions,
your heart is filled with joy,
you are learning to see
that in every corner,
on every wall,
there are lessons in them all
and you are free
to walk with confidence
through whatever door
before you
that leads to new Life.

You have traveled so far,
and you choose
again
today
to walk in the Light.

children
are not afraid
to let go
and forget everything
and start over again
and again,
laughing,
crying,
asking,
loving,
as they learn to live
with bravery.

BRAVE

This season
she is learning the art
of becoming,
unashamedly
stepping out
from behind the iron gate
she settled behind
long ago.

She is stepping
onto the cracked sidewalk
overgrown with wild green,
choosing to believe
out here in the unfamiliar,
in the open
she is free
to explore,
discover,
uncover
who she
is meant to be.

You do not have to live afraid.
You do not have to live
with the lie
that things will always be this way.

Today you can believe
things will come together
as they should,
all by grace,
for the better,
for the good.

AND IF YOU TRULY
WANT TO GROW,
MAKE A PRACTICE
OUT OF GRATITUDE:
THE DAILY
ART OF

CELEBRATING
THE LIFE UNFOLDING
BEFORE YOUR EYES.

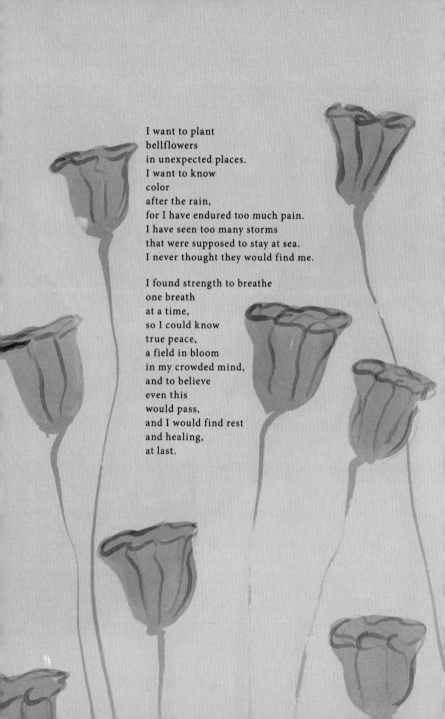

I want to plant
bellflowers
in unexpected places.
I want to know
color
after the rain,
for I have endured too much pain.
I have seen too many storms
that were supposed to stay at sea.
I never thought they would find me.

I found strength to breathe
one breath
at a time,
so I could know
true peace,
a field in bloom
in my crowded mind,
and to believe
even this
would pass,
and I would find rest
and healing,
at last.

FOR THE BODY

WHAT YOU DO

You might have a little fire in you,
a little rain,
a little thunder,
a little wind in your sail too.

You might have
a bit of your mother in you,
your grandmother,
her mother,
a beautiful old soul
you feel connected to.

And with all of these
many parts,
you were made to shine
unapologetically bright,
even when you do not know where to stand,
even when the lighting is not right.

So don't let anyone tell you
you have to have
the way you are
all sorted out
before you walk through your cave of doubt
into your life that is happening now.

And whether the way you come alive
is through your words,
your humor,
your tenderness,
your song,
now is the time to share
what has been in you all along:
a full-color soul
lined with gold
and a million stories
that make you
who you are.

Your small voice
has a way
of spilling into the rooms
where you thought there would be
no place for you.
Even when it is only
a word or two,
your small voice
has a way
of pushing through.

And if you happen to be
a little quieter,
and you sound differently from others,
the words you choose
resound with truth
all the same.

EVEN WHEN THERE ARE A
THOUSAND THINGS TO DO,
CHERISH THESE UNRUSHED
MOMENTS. MAKE ROOM IN
YOUR HEART FOR THEM.
THERE WILL BE MANY
MOUNTAINS TO CLIMB, BUT
ALWAYS MAKE TIME TO FIND
THE PASTURES WHERE YOU
can rest

her eyes are fixed
upward
where she is greeted by Everlasting Love
with Divine and open arms...
where she is reminded with every breath,
there is so much to who you are,
my dear, my dear,
there is so much more to who you are.

For all the times
you had to bend and break
and mold and shape
to meet someone else's expectations of you,
and for all the times you stood out

a little too much,
you were a little too different
or not different enough,

and you felt the gaze of those
who did not truly see you,
may you know this to be true:
their perceptions of you
may have crashed into your story,
like a floodgate falling
on your delicate heart,
but the water will only flow so far,
for their judgments do not hold enough weight
to find their way
beneath the surface
and into your inner layers.

LET RHYTHM
  GET INTO YOUR BONES
    AS IF THIS IS THE LAST TIME
    ON EARTH
      YOU ARE GOING TO HEAR THIS SONG.
OR GO AND SIT AGAINST THE WALL
  AND BE A WALLFLOWER IF YOU WANT TO,
    FOR TONIGHT MIGHT NOT BE THE END,
      BUT THEN AGAIN,
        WHAT IF IT IS?
YOU WERE MADE FOR THIS MOMENT.
  GET BACK INTO YOUR SKIN.
    DANCE AND CHERISH EVERYTHING,
      AS IF YOU MIGHT NEVER HAVE
        THE CHANCE AGAIN.

Come, and be free.
Go running into the clefts of the canyon
where the water pours.
Come afraid,
and come forth
as you are,
letting this rushing water remind you
of the life rushing through your heart,
life flowing through your body
showing you what it needs
is to know that being small in the canyon
does not mean you are too small to be.

For out here, in the wild,
you are agile
walking through your own uncertainty.

And that,
dear friend, takes bravery.

Put on your coat,
your boots,
your hat,
and grab your umbrella.

Go down to the city center
and wander into the cathedral.
Go where the sun is gone from the sky,
where your shadow climbs up the wall,
and be reminded
just how small,
just how small
you really are.

After all these years of going and going,
there is room to rest for a little while
in wonder
of the
majestic.

There is time to slow down
and stare up
at the blue, red, and hint of yellow
of a twentieth-century stained glass window,
a fading yet sacred art,
a masterpiece,
placed piece by piece
to create the kind of history
that comes to life beyond your eyes.

How do we know
how we were meant to spend every second of our time?
Were we really meant to rush with all abandon toward
some earthly hilltop finish line?

Or was God
telling us something
in those whispers to "be still,"
that all along,
it was necessary,
to slow down,
trust,
and heal.

Pause
and be unapologetically at awe
at this small piece of the world,
miraculously meaningful,
that took your trembling hand
and caught you by surprise.

When you get to go to that place
where the water
meets the mountain
and the mountain
meets the sky,
and you do not know where
to fix your eyes
because all of it,
absolutely all of it,
is one shade of blue—
this heavenly place—
this flicker in your soul—

When you get to that place,
go deeper into that blue.
Turn your eyes to
the water and the way
it reflects the mountain

and how the mountain
kneels to the sky
and how that long cloud moves
and that full-water ripples
and how in the heaviest of winds
you are still able to breathe,
and be reminded
you are living.

When you catch a glimpse of your reflection
and all you can see are the very things you fear,
do not be afraid, for light will meet you there.

And even though every flaw
has been illuminated here,
there is no reason to fear,
for there is beauty to be seen
amidst the scars that have marked you.

And whether they are easily seen
or you are the only one who seems
to notice they are there,
you are free to cast away those anxious cares
and fix your eyes on the wholeness
light revealed.

And it will not be easy,
facing the mirror each morning,
but perhaps you can be patient with yourself,
remembering that seeing the wholeness
of these scars
is a part
of getting to know
who you are.

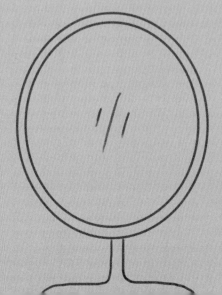

FOLLOW YOUR CREATIVE CURIOSITY.
NEVER LET THE ONES
WITH BRIMMING GALLERIES
AND WALLS AFTER WALLS OF THEIR LIFE'S WORK
STOP YOU
FROM PICKING UP YOUR PAINT BRUSH
AND DIPPING INTO THAT LITTLE SEA OF PAINT
THAT ;EXCITEDLY; AWAITS
WHAT WILL TAKE SHAPE.
REMEMBER
YOUR CHILDHOOD WONDER.

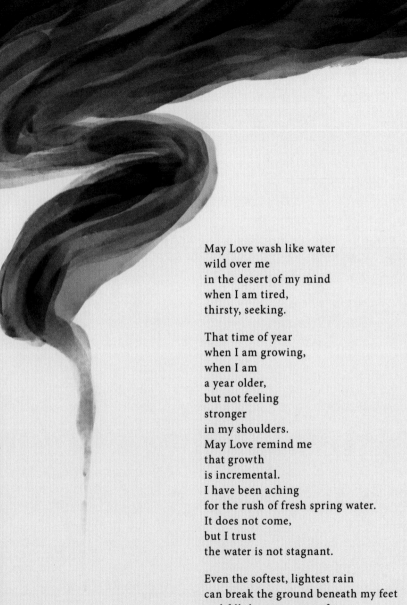

May Love wash like water
wild over me
in the desert of my mind
when I am tired,
thirsty, seeking.

That time of year
when I am growing,
when I am
a year older,
but not feeling
stronger
in my shoulders.
May Love remind me
that growth
is incremental.
I have been aching
for the rush of fresh spring water.
It does not come,
but I trust
the water is not stagnant.

Even the softest, lightest rain
can break the ground beneath my feet
and fill the very roots of me
with the tenderness I need.

If there is ever a day
when you are overwhelmed
by a crowd of expectations
and you are not ready
to throw yourself
on the line
in the way those above you
seem to want you to,
may you know this to be true:
you do not have to meet
every gatekeeper's
expectation of you
in order to show up
in a way that is true.

You do not have to
hide away
when the noise
of expectation
rings like an alarm
in your ears
drawing attention
to your fears
that maybe
you don't belong here . . .
When it's all too much,
grace is more
than enough
holding you
to remember
what is true
no matter what
they are asking of you.

We learn of our freedom when we are out in the open field.
We learn of our own growth with our feet planted in the grass,
and in the sun.
If we stand still enough,
we can catch a hint of gentle blowing wind
teaching us
again and again

seasons change, things happen,
but for some reason
we are here for every moment,
we are alive in it all,
and it all matters.

RATHER THAN WORRY
ABOUT CREATING A LIFE THAT WAS IMPRESSIVE,
SHE TURNED HER ATTENTION
TO CREATING A LIFE THAT WAS BRAVE.
SHE TURNED HER ATTENTION
TO BEAUTY OVER PERFECTION,
LOVE OVER COMPARISON,
AND TELLING A STORY OF GRACE,
INSPIRING OTHERS TO DO THE SAME.

Not everyone's strength looks the same.

Sometimes strength is grasping on to a jagged trail on the steep side of the mountain, with icy rain on your shoulders and wind on your back. Sometimes strength is continuing to push upward against the incline in pursuit of the highest peak. It's continuing the climb against heavy winds, as all of the traveled miles are wearing at your knees.

Sometimes strength is waking up and choosing to breathe another day.

Sometimes strength is getting out of bed.

Your "strong" might not look like her strong, and that is more than okay. You are not the same, so your strength will not look the same.

To breathe is brave.
Never underestimate the power
of an exhale.

There will be some nights
where you will look up and lose track
of all the stars you see,
and there will be some nights
you can't lift your head,
but in both
of those nights
and every other
night in between,
you are strongest
when you take
the time to breathe.

It takes courage
to live through heartbreak.
Breathing is no small feat.

Make time to set
THE TABLE
for other people, too.

When you find yourself falling into the pit of anxiety, remember the ladder of hope that reminds you there is no reason to be afraid. There is still a way out of this, and you are still capable—not perfect, but capable—and you have permission to try to climb again. Even if your hands shake, and your knees are weaker from the fall, you can still trade your fears of tomorrow with hope for today: the courageous decision to climb on anyway out of the pit of anxious thoughts.

There is no reason to live afraid.

IT IS MORE THAN OKAY
IF "GIVING YOUR ALL"
MEANS STARTING SMALL
AND TAKING IT DAY BY DAY.

EVERY BEAUTIFUL ROSE
BEGINS
AS A SEED
AND IS MADE PRECISELY THIS WAY.

There will be times
when the last thing
you want to do
is hear
that you have
to keep going.
The last thing
you will want to do
is feel
you have to keep pushing.

Let the breaths
leaving your body
second by second
remind you
how seconds soon
turn into minutes,
and these minutes
soon turn into hours
and hours
then turn into days
and even though you once thought
you were stagnant,
you have made it
a miraculously long way through the darkness.

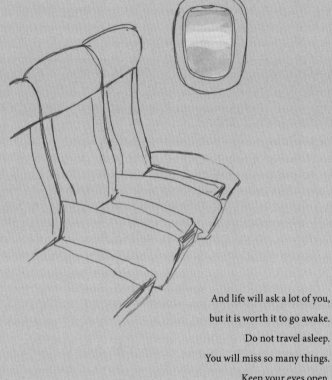

And life will ask a lot of you,
but it is worth it to go awake.
Do not travel asleep.
You will miss so many things.
Keep your eyes open.
Keep your heart open too.
There are so many things
the journey will reveal to you.

Maybe someday
I'll point my face
right into the mirror
and actually feel
layer by layer,
that I, too,
am beautiful.

Maybe
that day
can be today.
Maybe I can stop
looking for symmetry
and learn to
embrace the blemishes;
to accept me
for me,
without the pretense
of who I thought
I had to be.

Living in the moment

is learning how to live

between the big moments.

It is learning how to make the most

of the in-betweens

and having the audacity

to make those moments

just as exciting.

We think less of ourselves
because it feels safe.
If we don't build ourselves up,
then we won't be disappointed
when the sculpture
comes crashing down.

Our worth
is not delicate glass,
it is made of hope,
grace that lasts.
Through the good, the bad,
the I'm-afraids and I-don't-knows,
our worth withstands fire,
and we come forth as gold.

Take photographs of everything.
You never know how long these moments will be here.
Things are going to change.

I know it doesn't feel
that way now,
but they will.
You are not
going to be here forever.
Time will run
like wild winds
over the hills
impossible to capture,
and all you can do
is slow your pace
and hold
whatever you can
in your hands,
for things will not always be
the way they are.
So take photographs of everything:
ordinary things,
simple things,
between the door
and by the window things.
Light-ridden and shadow-heavy things.
Forever things.
Fleeting things.
Take photographs of everything.

You catch a glimpse
of beauty
in your conversations with him.
You will feel transported
to some new place
just by being around him.
Some people
create that spark.

I hope you know
the same way you see him,
you are entirely worthy
of being seen that way too,
because there is Glorious Light
inside of you,
and this Light,

this Light is a gift,
for you to receive,
embody,
and as a result,
begin to share
as Light
in the world
around you.

YOU ARE LOVED,
EVEN IN SOLITUDE.

YOU CAN FEEL AT HOME
IN THIS PRESENT MOMENT.
YOUR WORRIES
MAY BE OBSTACLES
BUT THEY ARE NOT
UNBREAKABLE WALLS.

AND WHEN SHE
TOOK HER SEAT
AT THE TABLE
AND SHE DID NOT QUESTION
IF SHE BELONGED,
SHE FOUND
SHE DID NOT HAVE TO BE
ALL SHE THOUGHT SHE'D HAVE TO BE
IN ORDER TO FEEL
CONNECTED
AND
RECEIVE
THE LOVE
SHE TRULY NEEDS.

DAILY

YOU ARE LOVED
AND WORTHY
OF LOVE

YOU ARE
BEAUTIFUL
INSIDE
AND OUT

YOUR PRESENCE
MATTERS

YOU CAN SLOW
DOWN AND
ENJOY THE
MOMENT

YOU ARE GOOD AT
LISTENING

HAHA!

YOU ARE
FUN TO BE
AROUND

AFFIRMATIONS

YOU KNOW HOW TO GET THINGS DONE

YOU ARE WORTHY OF COMMUNITY

YOU ARE NOT ON THE OUTSIDE LOOKING IN

YOU ARE IN TOUCH WITH THE STORY BENEATH YOUR SKIN

YOU ARE ENOUGH TO REACH YOUR FULL POTENTIAL

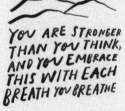

YOU ARE STRONGER THAN YOU THINK, AND YOU EMBRACE THIS WITH EACH BREATH YOU BREATHE

"BEING YOURSELF"
DOES NOT MEAN
YOU HAVE YOURSELF
ALL FIGURED OUT.
IT JUST MEANS
YOU ARE ALLOWED
TO 'SHOW UP'
WITHOUT THE
EXPECTATION
OF WHO SOMEONE ELSE
SAID YOU SHOULD BE.

Dive into the present moment
letting Light guide
your way.

You will certainly
face unknowns,
but you will not
face them alone.
All around you,
there are people
facing many of the same fears,
and many hide it,
without realizing it,
behind *how are you's*
and *I am fine's.*
And you can hone a listening ear
for the words beneath the words
the thoughts beneath the phrases
the feelings that do not reach their faces,
as you slowly begin to wake up

to the honest voice
inside of you
beginning to sing
with clarity and transparency
for yourself
and those around you.

BEFORE WE RUSH TO "DOING," WE MUST FIRST REST IN "BEING."

→BEING PRESENT WITHIN THE GRACE THAT ALLOWS US TO BE OUR UNMASKED SELVES, RIGHT HERE, WHERE WE ARE

LET THE SPLASH OF COLORS
IN THE SETTING SUN
REMIND YOU, AT THE END OF
IT ALL, YOU HAVE PERMISSION
TO BE UNDONE HERE.

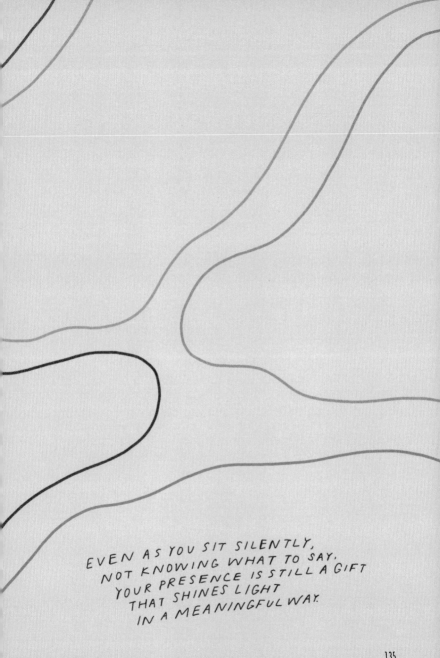

EVEN AS YOU SIT SILENTLY,
NOT KNOWING WHAT TO SAY,
YOUR PRESENCE IS STILL A GIFT
THAT SHINES LIGHT
IN A MEANINGFUL WAY.

LET TODAY BE THE DAY
  YOU ARE KIND TO YOURSELF
  AND FOCUS ON BELIEVING
    WHAT IS BEAUTIFUL AND TRUE.
AND THIS DOES NOT MEAN
  YOU IGNORE YOUR IMPERFECTIONS.
  IT MEANS, IN SPITE OF THEM,
  YOU BELIEVE
    THERE IS BEAUTY TO YOU.

SOME MOMENTS SCREAM THEIR SILENCE.
THEY SLOW US DOWN AND TEACH US
TO SEE WHAT LIES
BENEATH
THE LAYERS.

Your past
has shaped you
and is part
of who you are.
It has left wounds
forever stained on your skin.
No matter how many times
you have tried to forget
and let these stories fade away
by keeping them out of direct light,
it is okay
if there are still days
where you feel everything
and you have to take a moment
and say,
"In many ways,
this still affects me,
but I am leaning into the grace
that reminds me
I am free
to step out of the shadows
and still know peace here."

FOR THE SOUL

WHO YOU ARE

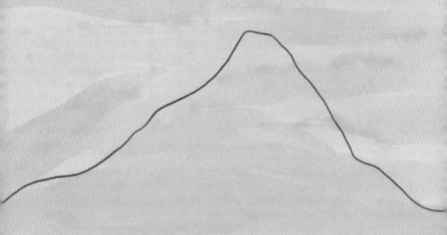

I stand in this valley
watching how the yellow-green grass
stretches up the blue mountain
against the coral-colored sky—

and I am reminded
no matter the times
my weary heart has tried,
nothing can wash away
the richness of these lands,
where silence is stronger than thunder.
My gratitude as steady as the hills,
I want to surrender to
gravity
remembering it is okay to feel small out here
as one of a billion divinely intentioned parts
of the morning hymn that has always been in you—
then sings my soul
How Great Thou Art.

And the thing about blooming is, nothing about the process is easy. It requires every part of you to stretch upward, with your roots firmly planted in the ground; and in the sun, and in the rain, and wind, you stand anyway, even against the pull of the soil. And through it all, one day you will see all along you were transforming. This took everything out of you, but the struggle was beautiful and necessary for your growth.

Amidst all the pressure
to keep going and to keep going,
may you also take time to learn the art of being;
being Loved,
being Held,
being Seen,
being in the Presence
of the One
who calls you
to rest.

For beyond your accomplishments
and your calendars, and your lists,
you were made with purpose and intention
to reflect Glorious Light
and to abide in Love
that reminds you
even in the pause
you are still
where you need to be.

No matter
how yesterday
unfolded before your eyes
and no matter the stacks of worries
burdening your mind
that have left you unsettled
or confused,
Light is still pouring in
reminding you over and over again
to surrender,
to let go,
for these troubles
are bound to shadows
that cannot survive in this new light.
Bask in these beams of sun
as you find your new beginnings,
a new way of seeing,

a grace-filled way
of living.

Oh, how steady
hope makes the soul
in the river rush of things
you cannot control.
For somehow through it all,
you have still been made whole.
Because as sure as the water
makes way
past the river stones,
so does hope carry you
past the depth
of your unknowns,
under fogged and white-gray skies
that demand
the most of tired eyes,
the sound of the rushing river
gently speaks:
all is passing,
truly passing.

What if all the imperfections
and the flaws
were only part of your story—
not the sum of who you are?
What if all along,
you were made to be beautiful,
and it was only the dirt from this broken world
that made you doubt your shining self?

And what if you were not alone,
as you once thought,
and when a friend
told you
she would be there,
she truly meant it?

What if for every time you were afraid,
you remember how you were brave,
and it only escaped your memory
because bravery is
natural these days?

Perhaps there are a million reasons
to never take the leap,
to never take the time to think
your presence means anything,
but I hope you know
there are more reasons to believe
this life is worth living for.

I hope you can look down
into that warped well of your imperfections
knowing whatever you find there
can never even compare
to the greatness in your soul,
shining wildly through.

THE THING ABOUT
SOWING SEEDS
AND WAITING
FOR THEM TO SPRING INTO THEIR BLOOM
IS THAT BEFORE ANY OF THAT BEGINS,
THE SOIL MUST BE PREPARED.
THE GROUND MUST BE BROKEN
BEFORE ANYTHING CAN GROW.

Where is strength found?
not only in the highs,

but neither only
in the lows.
It is found in the grasslands
and the wastelands
and the footpaths
in between them
in your laments
your anthems
and the quiet hours
in between.

strength
can arise
in these places,
unexpected.

In winter,
the trees are bare,
and the sun is glorious
casting silhouetted tree limbs.
The air blows cold around us.

We are seen.
We are known.

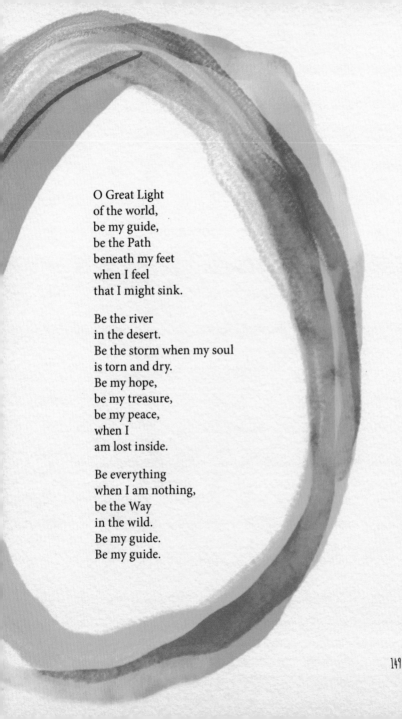

O Great Light
of the world,
be my guide,
be the Path
beneath my feet
when I feel
that I might sink.

Be the river
in the desert.
Be the storm when my soul
is torn and dry.
Be my hope,
be my treasure,
be my peace,
when I
am lost inside.

Be everything
when I am nothing,
be the Way
in the wild.
Be my guide.
Be my guide.

More than anything,
I hope you find your way home.
I hope you find
what speaks to your heart
like nothing else in the world
has spoken to you before.

As you sit in this terminal
hoping this new city
will be home,
the home that you've longed for
where your name will be safe,

where you will finally
belong—
as you're here
lugging luggage,
bumping shoulders
of others charging through
with apparently important things to do,
and you're berated by
the mechanic clattering of voices
citing numbers,
directions,
delays,
Alone
inching toward your unknown.

But take time
to listen
for the ever-present Voice
gently whispering,
"I'll guide you."
And may your love for traveling far
remind you of traveling grace
finding you here in the crowd
reminding you that you belong,
no matter where you are.

through all the times you fell
and all the times you ran
not knowing what was next
or where your feet would land,
and all that was lost in translation
of a language you could not understand,
even then,
you were known
and you were still
headed home.

in all that has changed
or stayed the same,
you have found comfort in the Voice
rising up above the noise:
"You are loved,
you are loved,
you are dearly, dearly loved,
and you're worthy of the journey
of being.
You're worthy of the journey
of finding home
in Me."

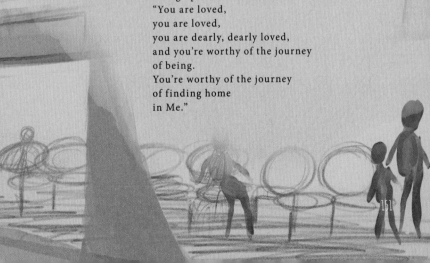

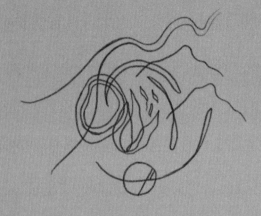

Step into the unknown and learn
as you go.

Walk through fire and
come forth refined
as gold
and journey on.

You have been made new,
and you see
nothing is ordinary.

SUNRISES IN AUGUST, HANDWRITTEN letters ON TUESDAY, AND AFTERNOON LULLABIES OF CARS DRIVING BY. THOSE THINGS ARE WORTH LIVING FOR TOO.

153

THE PEOPLE WHO SHINE BRIGHTEST
DO NOT HIDE THEIR ~~FAL~~ FAULT LINES.
THEY EMBRACE
THE LIGHT
THAT SHINES THROUGH.

You are being called beyond the shore
to a place you have never been before.
The water may be colder there,
and the ocean floor may seem too far,
but you are going to learn more of who you are.
So keep your eyes open
as you venture out today.
These waters are new,
but do not be afraid.
You are only going to grow here,
as your eyes and heart become open
to the process of becoming.

Let us leave room
for bold adventure
and wake up at dawn
in search of wonder.
Let us find joy
in the grit
of the wonderlands
and look for Light
in everything.
For all along,
we were made for this:
to step fully
into unknowns,
to know deep
within the night,
within the soul,
we were not meant
to go alone.
In every single
moonlit tree,
we were meant
to see those leaves,
and we were meant
to see the beauty
in the swaying arms
of branches.

So let us find rest
in these woods
so new to us,
knowing
this is where
we will learn
to grow
to love
to trust.

This is life.

You have been pulled into the fierce winds
carrying you over the barren hills,
leaving you bruised
on the shores of this rocky coast.

Your eyes have been reopened.
This life is broken.

Come now,
come falling
on your knees
on this bed of sand
where the stones have washed away
and the softened earth awaits,
take all the time you need
to be undone
and breathe.

Through all that is changing,
there are practices
we must hold on to:
wisdom,
love,
gratitude.
Gratefulness for how life's lessons
have shaped us,
and no matter
where the journey takes us,
we know we never go alone.

I want to be more than my ruins.
I want to firmly plant my feet
on top of the fallen columns of a
house I built out of my pride.
From death to life, I want to
know the Love way of rising up,
fully alive from the depths within
me, letting this new way of life
reshape my way of seeing.

WHILE YOU WAIT
FOR CLARITY
AND ANSWERS
TO PRAYERS
THAT HAVE PULLED ME
FROM MY SLEEP,
I WILL REST
WITH SWEET ASSURANCE
THAT DEEP WITHIN I HAVE THIS HOPE,
AN ANCHOR FOR MY SOUL,
"YOU WILL NOT SWIM THESE DEPTHS ALONE."

And as you start to ascend,
you feel the force of heavy winds
and for the first time,
you wonder if you should give up,
turn around,
and go back down
the mountain
and find a smaller hill to climb.

This is a broken place,
and you are treading on splintered ground,
trying to make sense of your progress,
and where you thought
you'd be by now.
And what was familiar is now too distant,
and what was unknown is now too close,
and you are wondering what to keep
and what to just let go.
But now that you're here, let it be.
Slow down and let it be.
Find new rhythms
in the silence
to cling to lasting peace,
knowing well within your soul
you will have the strength you need
to make it through
these unknowns.

Peace blooms
as you learn
    your soul is steady
        in chaos.

    Live
      as a stone
        in rushing water,
        grounded
            no matter the current.

She KNOWS
ETERNAL love
has PROVEN FAITHFUL,
AND she
is FOREVER grateful
FOR THE smallest prayers
that HAVE BEEN answered.

Decorate with flowers
or words
or music and
open the door for an old friend.

Just be there,
and listen,
without a word—
human to human,
heart to heart.

We are all
blooming,
and as we breathe this same air,
side by side,
we are reminded
at our core,
how similar we are.

What can we say
of this day?

It is here
this one time
and then
never will be again.

But we made time to see
the way autumn burns leaves
in the park
and
the thousands of footsteps,
hundreds of faces,
dozens of taxis,

making note of the little ways
life was pouring in.

When you get out there
and you feel far from home,
May you KNOW
there is grace
to come alive
IN YOUR UNKNOWNS.

There is freedom,
there is peace
to NOT be WORRied
about everything,
trusting fully
that hope will rise,
even in uncertainty.

A SINGLE FLOWER BEGINS THE GARDEN AS YOU WAIT FOR OTHER FLOWERS TO SPRING TO LIFE.
A SINGLE FLOWER BEGINS THE GARDEN AS YOU WAIT FOR OTHER FLOWERS TO SPRING TO LIFE.
A SINGLE FLOWER BEGINS THE GARDEN AS YOU WAIT FOR OTHER FLOWERS TO SPRING TO LIFE.
A SINGLE FLOWER BEGINS THE GARDEN AS YOU WAIT FOR OTHER FLOWERS TO SPRING TO LIFE.
A SINGLE FLOWER BEGINS THE GARDEN AS YOU WAIT FOR OTHER FLOWERS TO SPRING TO LIFE.
A SINGLE FLOWER BEGINS THE GARDEN AS YOU WAIT FOR OTHER FLOWERS TO SPRING TO LIFE.
A SINGLE FLOWER BEGINS THE GARDEN AS YOU WAIT FOR OTHER FLOWERS TO SPRING TO LIFE.
A SINGLE FLOWER BEGINS THE GARDEN AS YOU WAIT FOR OTHER FLOWERS TO SPRING TO LIFE.
A SINGLE FLOWER BEGINS THE GARDEN AS YOU WAIT FOR OTHER FLOWERS TO SPRING TO LIFE.
A SINGLE FLOWER BEGINS THE GARDEN AS YOU WAIT FOR OTHER FLOWERS TO SPRING TO LIFE.
A SINGLE FLOWER BEGINS THE GARDEN AS YOU WAIT FOR OTHER FLOWERS TO SPRING TO LIFE.
A SINGLE FLOWER BEGINS THE GARDEN AS YOU WAIT FOR OTHER FLOWERS TO SPRING TO LIFE.
A SINGLE FLOWER BEGINS THE GARDEN AS YOU WAIT FOR OTHER FLOWERS TO SPRING TO LIFE.
A SINGLE FLOWER BEGINS THE GARDEN AS YOU WAIT FOR OTHER FLOWERS TO SPRING TO LIFE.
A SINGLE FLOWER BEGINS THE GARDEN AS YOU WAIT FOR OTHER FLOWERS TO SPRING TO LIFE.
A SINGLE FLOWER BEGINS THE GARDEN AS YOU WAIT FOR OTHER FLOWERS TO SPRING TO LIFE.
A SINGLE FLOWER BEGINS THE GARDEN AS YOU WAIT FOR OTHER FLOWERS TO SPRING TO LIFE.
A SINGLE FLOWER BEGINS THE GARDEN AS YOU WAIT FOR OTHER FLOWERS TO SPRING TO LIFE.
A SINGLE FLOWER BEGINS THE GARDEN AS YOU WAIT FOR OTHER FLOWERS TO SPRING TO LIFE.
A SINGLE FLOWER BEGINS THE GARDEN AS YOU WAIT FOR OTHER FLOWERS TO SPRING TO LIFE.
A SINGLE FLOWER BEGINS THE GARDEN AS YOU WAIT FOR OTHER FLOWERS TO SPRING TO LIFE.
A SINGLE FLOWER BEGINS THE GARDEN AS YOU WAIT FOR OTHER FLOWERS TO SPRING TO LIFE.
A SINGLE FLOWER BEGINS THE GARDEN AS YOU WAIT FOR OTHER FLOWERS TO SPRING TO LIFE.
A SINGLE FLOWER BEGINS THE GARDEN AS YOU WAIT FOR OTHER FLOWERS TO SPRING TO LIFE.
A SINGLE FLOWER BEGINS THE GARDEN AS YOU WAIT FOR OTHER FLOWERS TO SPRING TO LIFE.
A SINGLE FLOWER BEGINS THE GARDEN AS YOU WAIT FOR OTHER FLOWERS TO SPRING TO LIFE.
A SINGLE FLOWER BEGINS THE GARDEN AS YOU WAIT FOR OTHER FLOWERS TO SPRING TO LIFE.
A SINGLE FLOWER BEGINS THE GARDEN AS YOU WAIT FOR OTHER FLOWERS TO SPRING TO LIFE.
A SINGLE FLOWER BEGINS THE GARDEN AS YOU WAIT FOR OTHER FLOWERS TO SPRING TO LIFE.
A SINGLE FLOWER BEGINS THE GARDEN AS YOU WAIT FOR OTHER FLOWERS TO SPRING TO LIFE.
A SINGLE FLOWER BEGINS THE GARDEN AS YOU WAIT FOR OTHER FLOWERS TO SPRING TO LIFE.
A SINGLE FLOWER BEGINS THE GARDEN AS YOU WAIT FOR OTHER FLOWERS TO SPRING TO LIFE.
A SINGLE FLOWER BEGINS THE GARDEN AS YOU WAIT FOR OTHER FLOWERS TO SPRING TO LIFE.
A SINGLE FLOWER BEGINS THE GARDEN AS YOU WAIT FOR OTHER FLOWERS TO SPRING TO LIFE.
A SINGLE FLOWER BEGINS THE GARDEN AS YOU WAIT FOR OTHER FLOWERS TO SPRING TO LIFE.
A SINGLE FLOWER BEGINS THE GARDEN AS YOU WAIT FOR OTHER FLOWERS TO SPRING TO LIFE.
A SINGLE FLOWER BEGINS THE GARDEN AS YOU WAIT FOR OTHER FLOWERS TO SPRING TO LIFE.
A SINGLE FLOWER BEGINS THE GARDEN AS YOU WAIT FOR OTHER FLOWERS TO SPRING TO LIFE.
A SINGLE FLOWER BEGINS THE GARDEN AS YOU WAIT FOR OTHER FLOWERS TO SPRING TO LIFE.
A SINGLE FLOWER BEGINS THE GARDEN AS YOU WAIT FOR OTHER FLOWERS TO SPRING TO LIFE.
A SINGLE FLOWER BEGINS THE GARDEN AS YOU WAIT FOR OTHER FLOWERS TO SPRING TO LIFE.
A SINGLE FLOWER BEGINS THE GARDEN AS YOU WAIT FOR OTHER FLOWERS TO SPRING TO LIFE.
A SINGLE FLOWER BEGINS THE GARDEN AS YOU WAIT FOR OTHER FLOWERS TO SPRING TO LIFE.
A SINGLE FLOWER BEGINS THE GARDEN AS YOU WAIT FOR OTHER FLOWERS TO SPRING TO LIFE.
A SINGLE FLOWER BEGINS THE GARDEN AS YOU WAIT FOR OTHER FLOWERS TO SPRING TO LIFE.
A SINGLE FLOWER BEGINS THE GARDEN AS YOU WAIT FOR OTHER FLOWERS TO SPRING TO LIFE.
A SINGLE FLOWER BEGINS THE GARDEN AS YOU WAIT FOR OTHER FLOWERS TO SPRING TO LIFE.
A SINGLE FLOWER BEGINS THE GARDEN AS YOU WAIT FOR OTHER FLOWERS TO SPRING TO LIFE.
A SINGLE FLOWER BEGINS THE GARDEN AS YOU WAIT FOR OTHER FLOWERS TO SPRING TO LIFE.
A SINGLE FLOWER BEGINS THE GARDEN AS YOU WAIT FOR OTHER FLOWERS TO SPRING TO LIFE.
A SINGLE FLOWER BEGINS THE GARDEN AS YOU WAIT FOR OTHER FLOWERS TO SPRING TO LIFE.
A SINGLE FLOWER BEGINS THE GARDEN AS YOU WAIT FOR OTHER FLOWERS TO SPRING TO LIFE.
A SINGLE FLOWER BEGINS THE GARDEN AS YOU WAIT FOR OTHER FLOWERS TO SPRING TO LIFE.
A SINGLE FLOWER BEGINS THE GARDEN AS YOU WAIT FOR OTHER FLOWERS TO SPRING TO LIFE.
A SINGLE FLOWER BEGINS THE GARDEN AS YOU WAIT FOR OTHER FLOWERS TO SPRING TO LIFE.
A SINGLE FLOWER BEGINS THE GARDEN AS YOU WAIT FOR OTHER FLOWERS TO SPRING TO LIFE.
A SINGLE FLOWER BEGINS THE GARDEN AS YOU WAIT FOR OTHER FLOWERS TO SPRING TO LIFE.
A SINGLE FLOWER BEGINS THE GARDEN AS YOU WAIT FOR OTHER FLOWERS TO SPRING TO LIFE.
A SINGLE FLOWER BEGINS THE GARDEN AS YOU WAIT FOR OTHER FLOWERS TO SPRING TO LIFE.
A SINGLE FLOWER BEGINS THE GARDEN AS YOU WAIT FOR OTHER FLOWERS TO SPRING TO LIFE.
A SINGLE FLOWER BEGINS THE GARDEN AS YOU WAIT FOR OTHER FLOWERS TO SPRING TO LIFE.
A SINGLE FLOWER BEGINS THE GARDEN AS YOU WAIT FOR OTHER FLOWERS TO SPRING TO LIFE.
A SINGLE FLOWER BEGINS THE GARDEN AS YOU WAIT FOR OTHER FLOWERS TO SPRING TO LIFE.
A SINGLE FLOWER BEGINS THE GARDEN AS YOU WAIT FOR OTHER FLOWERS TO SPRING TO LIFE.
A SINGLE FLOWER BEGINS THE GARDEN AS YOU WAIT FOR OTHER FLOWERS TO SPRING TO LIFE.
A SINGLE FLOWER BEGINS THE GARDEN AS YOU WAIT FOR OTHER FLOWERS TO SPRING TO LIFE.
A SINGLE FLOWER BEGINS THE GARDEN AS YOU WAIT FOR OTHER FLOWERS TO SPRING TO LIFE.
A SINGLE FLOWER BEGINS THE GARDEN AS YOU WAIT FOR OTHER FLOWERS TO SPRING TO LIFE.
A SINGLE FLOWER BEGINS THE GARDEN AS YOU WAIT FOR OTHER FLOWERS TO SPRING TO LIFE.
A SINGLE FLOWER BEGINS THE GARDEN AS YOU WAIT FOR OTHER FLOWERS TO SPRING TO LIFE.

I HOPE YOU SEE BEAUTY
IN FULL MOONS,
IN FULL BLOOMS,
AND IN THE SOUND OF RAIN.

I HOPE YOU FIND JOY
IN WHAT IS CHANGING
AND IN WHAT IS FAITHFUL
AND HAS STAYED THE SAME.

I will let life in.

I will not concern myself
gathering gold and silver
that can be taken from me.
I have to trust there is more to me
that goes beyond what I can see.
There is more to me
than what I know today.
I will stretch my hands up to the sky,
to say, "I am afraid but I will try,"
remembering
the sea was split in two
the veil was torn in two
so I could know deep
within my soul,
what it means to be Free.

I will not hold back,
for Love
has not
held back on me.

It is easy to admire
the grandeur of
mountains
while failing to mention
the lack of oxygen
at their altitudes.

But I find gratitude
climbing
a little closer
to the sky,
rising up
from the surrounding land.
I catch my breath
and I stand.

darling,
don't you know?
you don't have to
hold your breath
any longer.

REMEMBER,
REMEMBER,
YOU ARE ;MORE;
THAN FLESH AND BONES.
YOU ARE A SOUL
NEEDING GRACE
AND SALVATION
ON THE NARROW
JOURNEY HOME.

We stand tall in the high grass with wind on our backs and hope in our lungs.

We belong in this life.

There is a place for all of us here, by grace, there is a place for all of us here.

THERE IS MORE TO KNOW
AND MORE TO SEE,
AND ALL OF YOUR LIFE'S
MOST COLORFUL STORIES
WILL PREPARE YOU
FOR WHO YOU NEED TO BE.

No matter the doorkeepers
who told you that you were not welcome,
leaving you to wander
out into the margins
of a crowded city,
into the alleyways
late into the night—
beneath the wounds of their words,
there is still this lasting truth:
you are not doomed
to be lost forever.

You are free to find comfort.
You are free to be at rest
and be at home
in your wilderness,
exhaling
involuntarily,
free,
knowing there will be other doors
that will open up to you.
But in the meantime,
out here,
you have been found in the peace
in the piano music
drifting down
from the stairwell,
to carry on while waiting,
feeling secure
from here, within
right where you are.

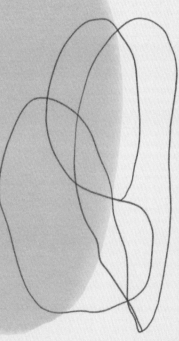

HOPE is a SMALL rebellion

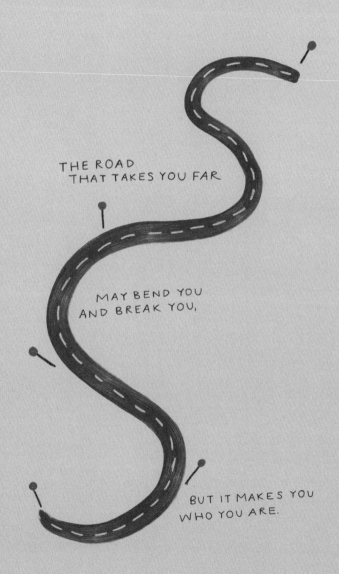

THE ROAD
THAT TAKES YOU FAR

MAY BEND YOU
AND BREAK YOU,

BUT IT MAKES YOU
WHO YOU ARE.

MOVE ON BUT HOLD ON TO BEAUTY AND TRUTH. DARKNESS HAS NO CHANCE AT DEFINING YOU

And may you raise your tired hands
in Spirit and in Truth
knowing deep within your soul
by grace, you'll make it through.
You'll look back on days like this
with blessed, warm relief
that in the darkness you still chose
to see the Light in everything.

You have endured
storms passing through,
and even though they shook you to your bones,
they did not stay with you.

Nothing more than yesterday's evening rain,
and though the ground is still damp in the morning,
this day is brand-new.

And it is okay if there are days
when you feel a little out of frame
and you hear rumbles of thunder
from where you thought the sky had cleared.
Though you cannot control the storm
it cannot hold you forever.
This is what the soul knows.

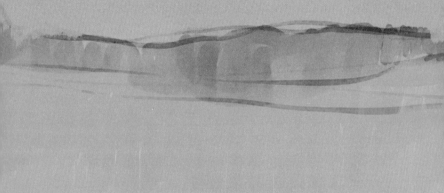

Light still fills the sky,

and though your heart gets heavy,
and your eyes have struggled
to find
the stars above
the streetlights,
you are free
to believe
Light is still
pouring in,
above,
around,
beneath,
within.

AND WHEN YOU GO
INTO THAT DEEP NIGHT
AND YOU FIND
UNBRIDLED FOOTPATHS
AND STARLESS SKIES,
MAY YOU KNOW
EVEN THEN
A FIRE BURNS WITHIN
AND WITH EVERY BREATH
IT IS REKINDLED
OVER AND OVER AGAIN.